Praise for *Simple Social Media*

"When you start a new project—or have to take over one—it's hard to have a consistent presence. Simple Social Media gives you a strategy, a content schedule, and helpful tips so that even small marketing teams can be consistent and authentic on social media."

— Joe Pulizzi, author of *Content Inc* and *Epic Content Marketing* and coiner of the term "content marketing"

"It's so rare that a book on social media hits the trifecta of useful, engaging, and actually strategic. But Annie has managed to do all three in one simple, and easily digestible book. 100% recommended for anyone who is trying to make their way in modern social media."

— Robert Rose, author of *Content Marketing Strategy: Harness the Power of Your Brand's Voice*

"Social media can be overwhelming. Annie breaks it down into manageable, logical, and doable steps that will help you take your social media game to the next level, all while making it fun to read with her witty '90s references."

— Brian Piper, co-author of *Epic Content Marketing*

"Finally—and I really mean it—FINALLY, a true social media expert brings real-world marketing wisdom to the average entrepreneur or business owner who knows they should be doing a better job sharing their story, adding value to their audience, and—wait for it—generating leads who are eager to engage. Annie's brilliant book gives you everything you need to master social media without driving yourself nuts. Read it, highlighter in hand, and follow Annie's smart advice straight to the bank. Yes, it's really that good."

— David Newman, bestselling author of
Do It! Marketing and *Do It! Selling*

"Simple Social Media is a must-read for anyone seeking to streamline their social media strategy and achieve real results. Whether you're a seasoned marketer or a newcomer to the digital world, Annie provides practical guidance and a breath of fresh air in the ever-evolving landscape of social media."

— Ross Simmonds, Founder of Foundation Marketing

Praise for the PAGER method

"Annie Figenshu's PAGER method gives small business owners a great step-by-step process to plan out content that will help grow followers and build community connection. This method helps transform the often overwhelming prospect of publishing content on social media into small, digestible parts. This book will be a great tool for anyone daunted at the prospect of starting their social media marketing, and will surely help them roll up their sleeves and get started."

— Margot Stephenson, Founder, Facts & Feelings Social Media Agency

"A genius new way to create social media content."

— *Marketing Made Simple Podcast*

"Simple, easy-to-execute ideas that can make all the difference in helping clients build their social media content. I'm excited to try this for myself!"

— Macy Robison, StoryBrand Certified Guide Program Director

"Engaging and relevant to every brand who is managing their own social media."

— Betty Lok, owner Betty Wonderful, LLC

"For an introvert like me, the PAGER method is really helpful and even fun to do."

— Cinthia Gonzalez, StoryBrand Certified Guide

"Annie gave us a really good methodology for working with our social media in a way that can help maintain momentum so it doesn't feel like we're starting over pushing that rock up the hill. Annie has one of the coolest ways to use the StoryBrand BrandScript that I've ever seen. And we're going to be implementing it for many of our clients in our social media."

— David McAndrews, Business Builder at Goalpost Group and Republic Healthcare

Simple Social Media

Build your brand with the PAGER method and have a presence without the pressure

Annie Figenshu

TILT
PUBLISHING

Tilt Publishing
700 Park Offices Drive, Suite 250
Research Triangle, NC 27709

For Abigail and Penny

You make every early morning
worth getting up for.

Contents

PART II
The PAGER Method

PART III
Implementing the PAGER Method

Introduction

"I hate social media." I hear that a lot.

Every time I give a keynote on social media marketing there's always at least one person who comes up to me afterwards and says that.

"But I'm gonna give this a try."

That's also what they say.

This book is for you if you hate social media. Or, you like social media, but hate spending a lot of time making social media posts. Or you spend a lot of time worrying about making social media posts. And you hate *that*.

This book is for you if you have to handle the social media for a group, a company, or an organization that you love. But this isn't your area of expertise. You just want more people to know about what you're doing. Because you're doing great work and more people would benefit from knowing about it.

You will learn how to make content faster. You will also learn how to mine what you already have for post ideas. And how to create a content stockpile that is continuously sending out posts on your behalf.

You will get a ridiculously simple method that builds relationships with people—real relationships—without spending hours every day on Instagram.

Basically, this book is for you if you like doing other things. And if you have other things to do.

The idea is to spend a few hours once a month and have your social media done for the next thirty days. You create posts, you vary them, you automate them. You move on.[1]

Because after a few weeks, that person who came up to me after the keynote will reach out to me again.

"I tried what you said. And it's so simple. It's just what we do now."

---

[1] Hopefully you move on to some other task that you like doing. Or maybe you move on to doing nothing. Hey, you do you.

I should probably point out at this point that you most likely have more followers than I have on social media. That may be so. But since implementing the method you will learn in this book, I have grown a network of followers, friends, colleagues, and collaborators. My company, Downstage Media, has a steady stream of leads, a client list we're proud of, and revenue has increased nearly 150% in the last year. So I'm not going to talk too much about growing your follower count as much as building a brand and a business. Because that's what I know. And that's what I do.

Please do get in touch and let me know how it's going. My email address is *annie@simplesocialmediabook.com* and I would love to celebrate with you the wins you are having from using the techniques in this book.

ANNIE Figenshu
February 24, 2023
New Jersey, USA

Note: Throughout the book, you'll find companion tools that can be downloaded, printed and shared by visiting *simplesocialmediabook.com*.

PART I

Why you need simple social media

Time to make the donuts

When I was a kid in the '80s, there was a popular commercial for Dunkin' Donuts.[1]

In this commercial, a somnambulant baker would stumble through the wee hours of the mornings lamenting, "Time to make the donuts."

And for a long time I felt that way too. "Time to make the social."

I was creating posts for four or five brands that would go out five times a week on two different platforms. That's fifty pieces of content *a week*.

---

[1] This is not product placement. But, Dunkin', if you're reading this, let's talk.

Every day I'd get up, get the kids to school, then create posts from about 9-2. Then I'd pick up the kids from school and when they went to bed I'd work another three hours. Making memes, videos, linking to articles. The whole thing.[2]

And the next day, I'd do it all again. "Time to make the donuts."

When I was on the ball, I'd be making posts for two weeks in advance.

But it would be easy to have a setback: A kid gets sick. I'd get sick. A snow day.

So sometimes I'd be making posts for the next day. Only to wake up and have to do it all over again.

I started hating three- and four-day weekends because it meant that the kids weren't going to be

---

[2] This is before TikTok and Reels. And I have to say, when those came out and it was all videos and pointing at things I was like, That's it. I'm out. Because nothing is more of a time suck for me than editing videos. And I know that AI can do a lot of that now.

in school and that was the only reliable childcare I had.[3]

I started to understand how truly relentless social media marketing could be.

I say this to let you know that I get it.

I know how it is to try to run your business and run your life too.

I get how hard it is to make sure you have enough to pay your business's bills while at the same time covering your bills at home while at the same time making sure your kids have their green t-shirts clean so they can wear them on St. Patrick's Day while at the same time making sure that you get your flu shots and your Covid boosters and you floss and recycle.

It's a lot.

I get it.

---

[3] Shout out to my friend and fellow working mom, Marie-Eve Turcotte, who often would help me fill in the childcare blanks by taking the kids for a few hours when they had random days off of school.

But what if we could make some parts of that a little bit easier? What if you could enjoy a three-day weekend instead of dreading it? Look, you may not feel like you can take away the flossing and the recycling part of your life. But if you're going to use social media to market your business, project, or product you can make the process a little more simple.

What's going on? (Scream from the top of your lungs)

Ask anyone involved in marketing where you should have a presence on social media and they will all tell you the same thing:

"Go where your audience is."

That makes sense.

Except the problem is, that on average, most social media users in the United States are using at least six platforms in any given month.[4]

Six! How the heck are you going to keep up with six social media platforms?

---

[4] According to We Are Social, Meltwater, and Data Reportal in their Digital 2023 United States of America report.

The fact of the matter is that you can't be everywhere all at once.

But the problem is, you've been told that you should be for so long that now, you think that you have to be.

Sure, that's possible for enormous companies that have huge marketing teams to handle their social media.

But you? You have a pretty lean marketing team.

And I'm using that term team pretty loosely since most of the brands that I work with have five or less people on their social media marketing teams. It's usually just one person.

So why are we expected to do all of this on social media?

New platforms are being added all the time. In 2010 your company was pretty much just on Facebook and Twitter. Now that's just the tip of the iceberg. You are faced with having a presence on Instagram, YouTube, LinkedIn. But you're also told to check out niche places like Quora or Reddit. And, then there are plenty of others that I'm sure have popped up and down by the time you're reading this.[5]

And it's not like you can just post a picture on Instagram, and a video on YouTube, and a link on LinkedIn. Nope, each platform is designed to make sure that you are posting all different kinds of content on each one.

But usually the parameters are a little bit different— so a picture that is the perfect size for LinkedIn doesn't look great on Twitter.[6] And if you have text with a link on Facebook, you can't do that on Instagram because Instagram doesn't like links.

And don't try to post a Reel with the TikTok watermark or else the algorithms will throttle the number of accounts you reach.

Features are being added to those platforms all of the time. So it's not just that you post your still

---

[5] A week before sending this to the editor Threads started up too. So there's that.

[6] When I began writing this book, it was called Twitter. It is no longer called Twitter. But it is highly possible that in between the time this book is written, edited, and printed it will change again and again. So, for clarity, I'm going to refer to it as Twitter. Or the artist formerly known as Twitter.

shots on Instagram and your videos on TikTok. You're expected to post a live video; a Story; a short, looping video; text with a link; text without a link on all the places.

So you have to make specific content for each platform and it is all such a time suck.

You are tired, you are exasperated. You feel like you are not doing it right. So maybe you don't do it at all.

You cringe when someone asks what your social media handles are.

Look, it's not your fault. You've been duped into thinking you need to be on all of the platforms all of the time. By the press that makes it seem like all you need is a social media account and your brand will make millions. By social media platforms that are designed to be addictive. By people trying to sell you books about social media.[7]

Who made these rules that said that you have to be on Pinterest, and Facebook, and Twitter, and

---

[7] Maybe not that last one.

Instagram, and TikTok, and BayLeaf, and Quora, and BeReal?[8]

You're not gonna take it anymore.[9] Instead, you're going to:

1. Choose one or two platforms strategically.
2. Create content that supports your goals.
3. Vary that content in different formats.
4. Automate that content.
5. Support your followers.

And this book is going to help you do just that.

Of course, the choice is yours. You can get with this, or you can get with that.

---

[8] One of those doesn't even exist but you didn't realize it because there are so many platforms out there.

[9] Now is a good time to mention that if you go to *simplesocialmediabook.com* you'll be able to access the PAGER Method Mixtape, a playlist of all the '80s and '90s songs mentioned in this book. Like Twisted Sister's "We're Not Gonna Take It."

If you ignore social media

Some people say to me, "My social media strategy is simple. I don't do it!"

I get it. Social media is relentless. Ignoring social media as a marketing channel, though, can have big consequences. You could miss out on building relationships with customers and turning them from a casual buyer to a fan for life who wouldn't buy from anyone else.

On the other hand, continuing to have a catch-as-catch-can social media strategy (which is really no social media strategy) or having an unsustainable social media presence is, well, unsustainable.

The following scenarios—and what happens if they're left unchecked—are what I often see from clients before they start focusing on their social media marketing.

Scenario #1

Posting takes time. Why bother? You don't even bother posting all that much anymore. Because when you *do* get all excited about posting, it takes up so much of your time that it's not sustainable long term. The problem is, then you spend so much mental energy with that niggling thought going through your head, "I've got to do something about my social media."

Scenario #2

You only post when you have something big coming up. Mostly because it takes so much time to come up with the kind of posts to make. And in the meantime, the algorithm penalizes you because the algorithm is passive aggressive against accounts that aren't consistent.[10]

---

[10] That last part isn't true. I mean, algorithms don't have feelings. But algorithms don't show your content to as many people if you haven't posted regularly. Think of the algorithm like a jaded gym rat on January 1st looking at you skeptically and saying, "Oh look. You're back. So lemme guess, you're gonna post all kinds of pictures and quotes and stuff? How long is that gonna last?"

Scenario #3

Your audience stays small because you don't know how to build relationships on social media. You don't meet new colleagues, potential clients, and new hires because you don't have a consistent presence and you don't have conversations with other people on social.

Scenario #4

Every time someone new takes over the social media marketing for your organization, you have to start from scratch again. So you get wildly inconsistent results depending on who has the keys.

Scenario #5

You put the youngest people on your staff in charge of the social media accounts because "they know this stuff better than I do." So you add it to their task list. They set up accounts on the platforms that they know. They usually post a lot of "fun stuff." And they spend a lot of time posting. But they don't get results.

All of these scenarios can have real consequences for your brand. If you do nothing, you will miss out on important opportunities. If you take action— even small ones—you will start to see results. You can relax about what you make, and how often you post it, because you're going to have a system in place. You'll start to build relationships with people that translate into increased revenue and opportunities. And you will be able to focus on the things in your life that you love.

I didn't want to do social media either

I didn't want to go back to making posts for other brands. But I had to.

At one point, I was making five posts a week on two different platforms for about six different brands. It was exhausting and it was relentless.

Burned out in January of 2020, I decided not to renew contracts with a couple of clients, a couple of them decided not to renew contracts, and the rest— mostly in the performing arts—stayed on.

But when the pandemic hit,[11] those clients weren't about to pay a monthly retainer for

---

[11] I'm talking about the 2020 Covid-19 pandemic. I really hope that in the time between my writing this and your reading this that another one didn't surface and I have to be more specific than that.

marketing something no one could attend for the foreseeable future.

So, when I got a call to handle the social media content for not one but two doctors' offices, I knew I had to take them on. My career was in the balance. My husband (an actor) wasn't performing and we had very little income.

I didn't really want to. My two kids were only going back to in-person school for half days at a time. I knew I was going to be rushing to get them to school, only to pick them up a few hours later. Then helping them get on their Google Meets, and making sure they knew when to transition from math to art class. My youngest was in second grade and barely knew how to type.

If I took on these clients, I'd have to figure out a way to make content more efficiently than ever while still supporting my family's needs, and without burning out.

I had to think of a new way to create content and schedule it out without it taking a lot of time and without having to bug the clients for photos and videos. Plus, I had to make sure the clients actually built their brands, connected with their audiences, and got a return on their investment.

And that's what led to the method you are about to learn here. A method to create, vary, and automate content so that you can go weeks without having to think about publishing social media content if you don't want to.

This is the method that I created and tested and honed for years. The method that I've shared with other social media marketers and taught to the social media teams at marketing agencies.

This is the method that has helped quintuple engagement, increase revenue, and build audiences.

This is the method that will make social media way simpler for you.

Eight social media marketing mistakes

These are the mistakes that most people come to me with. We're going to address them in this book so you can work through them to build your business on social media. By resolving them, you'll have better relationships with your audience and with your peers.

Which is your favorite mistake?[12]

Mistake 1: *You don't post at all.*

Resolution 1: Use the PAGER method to give you a strategy and cadence.

---

[12] Apparently, Sheryl Crow's was Eric Clapton. I know, right?

Mistake 2: *You put the youngest person in your office in charge of your social media because they are the youngest person in your office.*

Resolution 2: You put someone in the role who can be creative and consistent.

Mistake 3: *You post the same stuff at the exact same time.*

Resolution 3: You vary when you publish the content that you create.

Mistake 4: *You're on all the places.*

Resolution 4: You publish to one or two strategically chosen platforms.

Mistake 5: *You only post when there is something that you want your audience to buy.*

Resolution 5: You post a variety of content that has a mix of promotional, informative, and engaging content.

Mistake 6: *You don't set up specific times to respond to comments and DMs. So you're "always on" (and kinda burned out).*

Resolution 6: You designate times to reply to your audience so that you don't find yourself working around the clock.

Mistake 7: *You focus on building your social media audience and forget about building your email audience.*

Resolution 7: You focus on building your email audience while you build your social media audience.

Mistake 8: *You have a great social media presence, and a terrible website.*

Resolution 8: Your website is optimized so your audience knows what you offer, how it makes their lives better, and how they can get it.

By understanding these mistakes—and working to stop doing them—you can start to simplify your social and free up time for yourself so you can spend your time, energy, and budget on what lights you up.

It was Reels that got me—Reels and the pandemic, that is

There were three ways in which Covid changed my work and how I approach it:

1. I was forced to work more efficiently. With no more childcare for the foreseeable future, I no longer had uninterrupted hours to work. So I had to be hyper efficient in the work that I did.

2. Reels took me off Instagram. TikTok[13] was a welcome distraction for millions of people and took off like wildfire. Meta copied TikTok with its Reels format and suddenly every content creator had to start dancing in videos and pointing at things to the sound of a robot voice. I didn't want to do that, mostly because video

---

[13] RIP musical.ly

editing takes me a very long time. So I dropped Instagram from my reperoire. And I realized that it was way easier to only be on two social media platforms.

3. I stopped using all social media for about six months. 2020 was a bleak time for many, and most of my clients were in the performing arts. No one had any work. And no one knew when they were going to work again. And, well, it was pretty sad. So I stayed away from social media. And when I tiptoed back to it, I had a completely different way of using it.

I'm sure that Covid forced you to reevaluate some element in your life in some way. For me, I learned that you have to be more efficient with content creation. You need to focus on only two platforms. And how you can show up on social media to get results.

Don't worry. Be happy?

Social media can bring up some strong feelings. And when it comes to running a brand, there's just a lot of worry:

Worry that you haven't posted in a while.

Worry that your post wasn't good.

Worry that people won't react to your post.

Worry that your strategy isn't working.

Worry that you didn't use hashtags.

Worry that you used the wrong hashtags.

Worry that a troll is going to comment.

Worry that a bot is going to comment.

Worry that no one is going to comment.

Worry that no one will see the post and all this worry is pointless.

And the double whammy: Worry that worry can turn into anxiety. And that anxiety can turn into dread.

No wonder so many people say that they hate social media. They hate feeling like they aren't good enough and that they can't keep up.

But to paraphrase Bobby McFerrin: in social media, expect some trouble. But when you worry, you make it double. Don't worry, be happy.

Tip: Most brands don't need to go viral. They don't need to do what's trending. Brands simply need to show up consistently on one—maybe two—social media platforms while building an email list.

Ways to minimize social media dread

Question: When you think about your brand on social media, do these feelings ever come up?

- Unworthiness
- Anxiety
- Fear
- Dread
- Worry

If you are feeling dread about your social media accounts (or at least anxiety, or at the very least worry), there are some ways to combat it.

I think of it a lot like meal planning. If you're scrambling to put a meal together every day, you're probably going to feel anxious and nervous about it.

But when you have a plan—and you take the time to work that plan—you may still feel busy, but you won't feel harried. You won't feel like your hair is on fire. And you won't feel social media dread.

Additional ways to cut down on social media dread:

- Reduce the number of platforms you are posting on.[14]
- Have a set schedule of the kinds of posts that you're going to publish every week (keep reading for what those kinds of posts will be).
- Create content in batches.
- Automate your scheduled posts (we'll get into what that is and how to do it in upcoming chapters).

These feelings are completely normal. And ones that you can turn around.

For now, I just want you to notice that they're there. And they're not helpful. And they've got to go.

And you're going to banish them.

---

[14] Seriously. Jay Clouse, founder of Creator Science, recently posed the question to a room full of content creators, "Is it easier to get all As when you take five courses or one?" The answer is clear. And he's 100% correct on this point.

Two platforms— at most

Unpopular opinion alert:

You don't need to be everywhere on social media.

You don't even need to be most places on social media.

You just have to pick one—maybe two—platforms to build your brand on.

I know, I know.

But what if my audience is in all of these places? Don't I have to be in all of these places?

No. You don't. My guess is that you have a very small marketing team. And I'm using that term team loosely since most of the brands that I work with have five or less people on their social media marketing teams. Making the kind of content that will get in front of your audience on all of those platforms will eat up all of the time in a week.

I have a scheduler that can take all of my content and put it out on every platform. Can't I just do that?

Sure. But my guess is that you are still going to have to tweak your content to be different sizes and lengths to fit each platform. And that takes time that you could be spending building relationships with more people on one or two platforms.

But this new app is so popular. Don't I have to check it out?

Sure! Check it out! But don't change your entire social media strategy to include it until you are sure that it's going to put your brand in its best light.

Choose two—at most.

If you have a marketing team of less than five people, you are spreading yourself too thin by trying to build an audience on more than two social media networks.

Here's why:

Most likely you are also creating longer form content in other places as well. Maybe you also have a:

- Blog
- Podcast
- YouTube channel
- Email newsletter

If that's the case, then you don't need to double that by having a widespread social media presence.

As mentioned before, but it bears repeating: Jay Clouse of Creator Science has said that it's like school: It's easier to get straight As taking one class than taking five.

According to research done by *The Tilt*,[15] even people who earn an income from content creation are building their audiences on only four unique channels.

Here's how this concept works in my world. And, as a reminder, I'm a one-woman show content creator. I own a social media marketing agency, but I create almost all of the content myself.

---

[15] 2023 Creator Economy Benchmark Research.

As of this writing, I'm currently building an audience using these channels:

- Instagram
- LinkedIn
- An email newsletter
- A blog

So choose two social media platforms (at most) to focus on. And it is okay if you only want to pick one.

Tip: If you are going to grow your audience on two social media platforms, avoid two that are owned by the same company. For example, Meta owns Facebook, Instagram, and Threads. It's important to diversify.

Keeping up with the changes is easier on only two platforms

Another reason why I support being on only two social media platforms—besides how it's just going to simplify your social media in general—is this: It's easier to keep up with all of the changes that social media platforms throw at you when you are only focused on one or two.

Here's how I think of it: Let's imagine you've got four or five kids.[16] I would imagine, it would be hard to keep up with all of the doctor appointments, school responsibilities, and after school activities that all of your kids have going on. Like, sure, you can get to Back to School night every year, but most

---

[16] Hey, maybe you do. In which case, if you are handling that then maybe you can be on three platforms.

likely someone's not getting to the dentist twice a year, amirite?

At some point you just have to say, "Sure, it would be cool if you could do tap classes, but your brother is taking swim lessons at the same time, and I can't drive you across town to get there. So we're just not doing that."

Same thing with social media platforms.

Social media platforms are constantly adding and subtracting features. Sometimes they're small tweaks—like allowing you to save and download your Instagram Live videos—sometimes they're big additions, like Stories.

It's hard to keep up with those changes if you are stretched too thin. And a reminder: if you are on more than two social media platforms and you have a marketing team of less than five people you are stretched too thin.

And when you can't keep up with the changes, then you can't capitalize on them. And that can be a missed opportunity.

But when you're only on two social media platforms and they add or subtract a feature? No big deal. You can handle that. It's simple.

Getting to know your brand's Norms is easier on only two platforms

In the '80s and early '90s there was a TV show named *Cheers* that took place in a Boston bar. The lyrics to the theme song[17] mentioned it being a place "where everybody knows your name."

Every time the character Norm walked in, the bartender, Sam, and everyone else in the bar would turn to him and shout his name, "Norm!"

And that's why you should only be on two platforms.

Because if your account is that Boston bar, and you are the bartender, you want to get to know your

---

[17] Why aren't there theme songs like there used to be? They were so catchy and fun and such tight songwriting!

Norms. And it's easier to do that when you only have one or two bars to tend.[18]

Also, it's worth noting that not only did the bartender at Cheers know Norm; all of the other patrons did too.

When you can get to know your individual audience members from their comments and the conversations that you spark with them, your other audience members will start to know them too. This is the essence of building a community, and this is what social media is all about: being social.

Cheers!

---

[18] Great Norm joke:

"How does a beer sound, Norm?"

"I don't know, Coach. I usually finish them before they get a word in."

Simple Truth:

You don't have to
be everywhere.
Just be authentic
where you are.

Stats on why it's time for simple social media

By now you've eliminated the stress of actually creating and posting content on more than one social media platform. I also hope that you've eliminated the anxiety of thinking that you need to be on more than one platform.

So from now on if there is a new, buzzy platform that pops up, you can just say to yourself, "I'm not going to do that right now." You can look into it. You can check it out. See what kind of content that people are creating on it. Get the *vibe* of the place. But you don't have to commit to having a social media presence there.

Building a social media account takes time. Marketers know that, but most business owners don't.

Social Media Examiner's 2023 Industry Report has data to prove that "at least 50% of marketers who've been using social media for two or more years report it helped them improve sales." Only 29% of the marketers surveyed say that sales have improved in less than twelve months.[19]

If you flip that stat around, it means that 71% of marketers said that sales improved in less than a year. And that number only lowers to 50% after two years. So social media marketing is a long game.

So, something I want you to remember is that it will take you awhile to build your audience.

And if you have been posting for *years* on social media and feel like you haven't gotten any traction, you are not alone. This happens to thousands of brands. When you're just publishing posts and hoping that your audience is going to see what you put up there without a real strategy to respond or engage, you're not going to get anywhere.

When you start focusing on one or two platforms you will start to see that you get results. But you've got to focus.

---

[19] socialmediaexaminer.com/social-media-marketing-industry-report-2023

You have to look 1-2 years into the future and think to yourself, can I really sustain this? Is this sustainable? *Who* is actually going to create this stuff? And who is going to interact with the people who comment or direct message my accounts? Who's going to look at the stats and see what's working and what isn't?

There is a lot to running a social media account, and you want to make sure you have a sense of what you're in for. For a list of questions to ask before starting any social media platform, get the resources at *simplesocialmediabook.com*.

Six social media platforms that were huge. Until they weren't

(Not really in chronological order)

1. Friendster
2. MySpace
3. Google+
4. Vine
5. Tumblr
6. Periscope
7. Meerkat
8. Clubhouse

A friendly reminder to be on two social media platforms that aren't owned by the same company because you never know when they're going to disappear. Also, a reminder to build your audience on email so that if any and all social media platforms go away you can still reach your audience.

How to algorithm-proof your audience

Growing your email list is super important and a key reason to create social media content. Here's why: Remember that list of apps that were popular until they weren't? Every single one of those apps had influencers that lost huge audiences because they only built a following on that platform.

So, when Vine just—poof!—disappeared one day? All of those influencers had suddenly lost all of their followers. They had no way to tell them, "Come find me on Instagram." Or better yet, "Subscribe to my email list so you can always find me."

Those influencers had to start from zero on a new social media platform.

In the blink of an eye your account can get taken away, a platform can get shut down, the algorithm can change. Just ask Thea-Mai Baumann.

Baumann started her Instagram account in 2012 with the handle @metaverse. In 2021—nearly ten years later—her account was "blocked for pretending to be someone else." Just a few days earlier, Facebook had announced it was changing its name to Meta.

"This account is a decade of my life and work. I didn't want my contribution to the metaverse to be wiped from the internet," she said. "That happens to women in tech, to women of color in tech, all the time," added Ms. Baumann, who has Vietnamese heritage.

Baumann told her story to the *New York Times* and a month later her account was reinstated with an apology from Instagram. But she nearly lost a decade's worth of her life and her art.[20]

In the summer of 2023, Gene X Hwang met a similar fate when his @x account, on the app formerly known as Twitter, was taken from him when the company rebranded. He was offered a new handle,

---

[20] *bbc.com/news/technology-59638311*

some X merch, and a tour of the offices. All of his data and followers would be moved to his new handle.

Hwang told *Tech Crunch*, "It would have been nice for them to compensate for it since it did have a lot of value to me, but things are what they are."[21]

Indeed.

By collecting your audience's email addresses, you are not only algorithm-proofing your audience, you're billionaire-proofing it.

---

[21] techcrunch.com/2023/07/26/twitter-now-x-took-over-the-x-handle-without-warning-or-compensating-its-owner/

The Christmas I learned the true meaning of social

On December 27th, 2020, I took a meeting with a Tony Award-winning Broadway composer whose work I'd known and admired for decades.

Andrew Lippa had been on my list of people I'd wanted to work with. So I made a point to keep up with him and his projects on Twitter. (Twitter lists were an amazing feature of the platform, and a great way to clandestinely categorize potential collaborators.) And right around Christmas he tweeted how he wanted to start an initiative to raise money to help theater people who had to move out of the city because they'd lost their jobs in the pandemic and couldn't afford rent.

I saw the tweet, responded how I'd be happy to help with marketing, and six months later Lippa, Tony nominee Kyle Jarrow, Kara Unterberg, Lilli Cooper[22] and I launched the Places Please Project. We raised over $100,000 in just a few weeks and were able to help theater workers come back to New York City after having been displaced in the pandemic. That would not have happened, if I hadn't started a new social media strategy the summer before.

In the summer of 2020, I was pretty sad about, you know, the whole state of the world and my career, and wracked with worry. So "creating content" wasn't really something I was up for. But I did want to connect with other people. So I just started slowly reading Twitter again.

And then slowly I started replying. I wouldn't post anything of my own, per se. But I would solely respond to people.

And when I did respond to them, I would just try to say something nice. I mean, we were all collectively being traumatized by a pandemic so why not be nice, right?

---

[22] At one point I realized I was the only one of the group of us who hadn't been nominated or won a Tony award. Cool, cool. No biggie.

Sometimes, I would retweet what someone else had said if it seemed especially inspiring or entertaining or informative. And I would add some positive two cents.

I did that for about ninety days. Just replying and sharing and supporting. And guess what happened?

After nearly ten years of being on Twitter, I actually started to get to know the people that I was following because I was finally taking the time to listen to them without wanting anything from them.

I didn't care if they followed me. I didn't care if they "liked" my tweets. I didn't care if they retweeted my tweets. All I cared about was listening to them and helping them feel supported.

Of course, then, my Twitter account grew. The number of accounts I reached increased over 296% in ninety days.

Because of that initiative, I was able to build relationships with people in the industry that I've always wanted to meet. None of that would have happened if I were still using Twitter the way I always had.

You will not go viral with the PAGER method

Just want to manage some expectations here.

You will not go viral with the PAGER method and the techniques in this book.

Look at my social media accounts—I have a tiny following. But I do have an engaged audience of followers, prospects, allies, customers, and colleagues. I have a robust pipeline of leads. And my revenue has nearly tripled in the past three years.

So, even though I don't have the big vanity metrics, social media is doing exactly what I want it to do for my business.

So it's not so much about followers. It's more about making yourself available on social media and responding quickly. Much like a pager from the '80s and '90s.

Think of your social media presence like a lobby in an office building. When you enter the lobby, you want it to be clean and professional. You don't necessarily need a "wow" factor going into the lobby, but you want it all to make sense. You want to feel confident that you can hang out in the lobby and do business with the company.

That's the kind of social media strategy that the PAGER method is.

It's not intended to turn you into an influencer. Or to make you go viral. But it is intended to make it clear to your audience what your brand is, and what it does for them. So they can decide if they want to follow you. Then they can decide if they want to engage with your content—and ultimately decide if they want to work with you.

Like all other content marketing efforts, this is going to take at least six months to a year of consistent posting, commenting, and sharing to truly see results.

Going back to Social Media Examiner's 2023 Industry Report, most marketers (78%+) who've been using social media marketing for one year or longer report it generates exposure for their businesses. That number drops to 59% when they've been using social media marketing for less than 12 months.[23]

The bottom line: This is a social media strategy that is sustainable for your business, but it's a long game.

---

[23] *socialmediaexaminer.com/social-media-marketing-industry-report-2023*

If you get this whole "simple social media" thing right

When you decide to take action for your social media marketing, you'll start to see some pretty exciting results. The following scenarios have actually happened to me or Downstage Media's clients once they committed to simplifying their social media and using the PAGER method.

Scenario #1

One client I was working with was able to make ten social media posts in thirty minutes, which he then could schedule out for the next ten weeks. I spend maybe an hour or two every week on social media content—and I have twenty-four posts going out every week. Rarely do I have two posts going out on the same platform and at the same time.

Scenario #2

One client—an audiobook reader—was able to corral and energize her audience so much that they created their own Facebook fan group devoted to her.

Scenario #3

You can go on vacation, take care of a sick household,[24] and attend a conference for a few days without worrying about your social media posts because you know you already have them on autopilot.

Scenario #4

You know what to post and how often without second guessing yourself.

Scenario #5

Your website gets more views because you are pointing your audience towards worthwhile links on it.

---

[24] You know how it is. It's not just a sick kid. It's a sick *household* because everyone gets it and then there's cleaning, and laundry. It's a whole thing and it can set you back days.

Scenario #6

Your boss has you handling the social media for the accounting firm you work at. Even though you don't know a whole lot about accounting, you can easily make posts to publish that are still relevant to your brand and your audience—and you can make them in record time.

Scenario #7

You're able to mine existing content so you don't have to invent so much to post.

These are all real world examples of what can happen when you have simple social media and you use the PAGER method and the techniques in this book.

PART II

The PAGER Method

The simplicity of the pager

"I come back stronger than a '90s trend."

— Taylor Swift

The '90s seem to be everywhere these days, don't they? I saw a seventh grader wearing a Nirvana t-shirt the other day. I asked her what her favorite song was. She couldn't name one. She just thought the shirt was cool. Wild!

When people talk about the past, they often speak about it as a simpler time. And since this book is all about simplifying, it seems only fitting that we would talk about a very simple communication device: the pager.

If you were a teen in the '90s, you would know what a pager was. Grown-ups joked that drug dealers had them.

Doctors actually had them. And teens wanted them.

I'll say this: one of the girls in my high school class who had a pager went on to be a cast member on *The Real World*[25] on MTV.[26] So, I mean, need I say more? Pagers were cool.

A pager—also known as a beeper—was a small electronic device that you would wear that was about the size of a deck of cards. When someone called you, it would beep, and that person's phone number would flash on its tiny screen. You would then walk yourself to the nearest payphone or landline and call the person back at that number.

---

[25] Children, *The Real World* was one of the first reality shows. It was on MTV and had seven strangers picked to live in a house to see what would happen when people stop being polite and start being real. True story.

[26] Again, for you young ones, MTV was a cable channel that was centered around music until it became centered around reality shows. *The Real World* was the reality show that started to turn the tide of its programming and usually put beautiful people in a cool house or apartment. With lots of alcohol. And, guess what? Drama ensued.

74

Not a lot to the pager. You'd look down, see the phone number, and call the person back. Simple.

The pager inspired the social media strategy I'm about to lay out to you. You wear it every day. Someone reaches out to you. You respond to that person.

At its essence, that's what you're doing with social media. You show up consistently. Someone responds to you. You reply to that person.

So let's dive in to the PAGER method in order to make social media simpler for your brand.

Consistent, weekly (monthly? daily?) categories

With the PAGER method, the social media posts that you create fall into one of five categories.

You publish one piece of content from each category. Using this as a guide you will post four to five times a week.

And for those platforms that require you to be a maniac,[27] you can post four to five times a day. Once from each category.

How often you post is up to you. That said, I have found that working your way up to posting four to five times a week is a cadence that keeps you

---

[27] I'm looking at you, Twitter, X, whatever you're calling yourself now.

showing up consistently, keeps the algorithms happy, and keeps you on your audience's radar.

Like wearing a pager every day.

Each letter of PAGER stands for a different category of content that you will create posts for. It breaks down like this:

- **P**romotional
    - Point audience towards a sale.
    - Increase sales and subscribers.

- **A**rticles
    - Point audience toward long form content.
    - Increase traffic.

- **G**eneral
    - Give informational, inspirational, entertaining bits of content on the platform.
    - Increase relationships with empathy and authority.

- **E**ngagement
    - Nudge your audience to interact with your brand.
    - Increase reach.

- **R**andom
  - Use any content from the past.
  - Keep algorithms happy.

Let's get into more detail on each one, why they are necessary to support your business, and how you can create content for them.

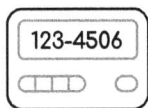

123-4506

Promotional

Articles
General
Engagement
Random

The PAGER method:
Promotional content

We've all seen it: social media accounts that just post about themselves all of the time. It's kind of gross. Normally we just scroll right on by, until eventually, they don't even turn up in our feeds anymore. You know you don't want your brand to be like that.

On the other hand, you've got a business to run. And as Diddy, Biggie, and the rest of the family have told us time and time again, it's all about the Benjamins. And you need customers. And social media helps you connect with those customers and find new ones.

It can be confounding trying to figure out the right amount of self-promotional content that will let your audience know what you offer without turning your account into a constant commercial. Gary

Vaynerchuk,[28] in his book *Jab, Jab, Jab, Right Hook,* says you should post promotional content one out of every four times. Many of the social media agencies that I have spoken with apply an 80/20 rule where 80% of the posts are informational, entertaining, or inspiring and 20% are promotional. So in putting together the PAGER method, I came up with one out of every four or five posts being promotional.

Here's what I mean by a Promotional post: Content that directly asks for the sale and points the audience to a specific action that's going to grow your business counts as Promotional.

Promotional content falls into three main categories:

- Sales
- Initiatives
- Events

When I would create social media content for clients, their business goals usually revolved around one of these three elements.

---

[28] A fellow New Jersey business owner.

Sales

When you have a sale coming up, or anything that's a "limited time offer," you can talk about it on social in a Promotional post. Think about Black Friday sales. Cyber week sales. Or a summer sale. Sales usually involve a date range of some sort.

Most small, independently-run brands publish these kinds of posts too often or not at all. Often, it's because smaller brands don't think along these lines. They are so caught up in the day-to-day of running their businesses that they don't think about a big holiday season that's coming up. Or they don't look to how their services map to a season and capitalize on that. They're just too busy. At Downstage Media we start talking to our clients in September about their Black Friday / Cyber Monday plans.

Exercise: What is a sale that your company has coming up—or could have coming up—in the next ninety days? Be as specific as you can:

_____

_____

_____

_____

_____

_____

To see examples of Promotional content, head to *simplesocialmediabook.com.*

Initiatives

"You know, we offer [this service] and no one ever buys it. We need to let more people know about it."

That's what I would hear from a client of mine, a doctor, who offered a whole host of treatments. But most of his patients only came in for one or two.

It was important, then, that his social media audience knew about all of the services that he offered. But if we talked about all them every time we did a Promotional post, it would get confusing for the audience. So we came up with seasonal initiatives.

Each quarter, sometimes each month, he and his team would come up with a different treatment that they wanted to highlight on social media. I made sure that we put that service into the social media content mix during that time.

Unlike a sale, which is driven by external dates, an initiative is driven by your company's internal goals. As an example, if you have a freebie[29] that you've created to increase your email subscribers, then your company may have an initiative to get more people to take advantage of it. So you need to make content around it.

Initiatives are best thought through with your whole team at a quarterly meeting. So the next time that you have one, think about a service or a product that you offer that you want to increase sales for. Then you and your team can build social media content around it.

If you don't have official quarterly meetings, then at the end of each quarter take some time to think about the Sales, Initiatives, and Events that you have coming up in the next ninety days.

---

[29] Sometimes called a lead generator in the marketing biz.

Exercise: What is an Initiative that your company wants to highlight in the next ninety days?

_____

_____

_____

_____

_____

To see examples of Promotional content that highlights a brand's initiatives, head to *simplesocialmediabook.com.*

Events

Events are just that—events that you have going on in your business that you need your audience to show up for.

Events can be:

- Shows
- Webinars
- Open Houses
- Workshops

Anything that you want other people to attend.

Unlike sales, events have a date, and a time as well.

Exercise: What is an Event that your company has coming up in the next ninety days?

_____

_____

_____

_____

_____

To see examples of Promotional content that highlights a brand's events, head to *simplesocialmediabook.com.*

The PAGER method:
Articles content

In 1998, Ani DiFranco told us most of what we needed to know about long form content and how audiences consume it. In her song "Little Plastic Castles" she says, "I picked up a magazine / which is every magazine. / I read a story / then I forgot it / right away."

And this, dear reader, is why you can reuse content.

The A of PAGER stands for Articles. And I really mean long form content—like articles—that you've created or been in.

Articles content encompasses:

- Articles you have written
- Articles you've been featured in
- Blog posts you've written

- Curated content
- Podcast episodes you've made
- Podcast episodes you've been a guest on
- Videos that you've created
- Videos you've appeared in

Articles content is meant to combat another issue that I hear from people:

"Social media doesn't drive traffic."

Too many people say that, without even bothering trying to point their cars in the right direction.[30] Or any direction for that matter.

They post a link the day their blog post comes out and then they're surprised that people aren't clicking on that link in droves.

"Create once. Distribute forever."

— Ross Simmonds

---

[30] The phrase "driving traffic" is a car metaphor, right?

I recommend that you not only send out a link on the day that the article / episode / post publishes, but that you regularly and repeatedly distribute the piece. You are going to hit them, baby, one more time. So if you were a guest on five podcast episodes, then you cycle between posting those five podcast episodes once a week, every time that you post Articles content. And when you run out, you start from the beginning again.

Or you add in a blog post that you wrote. Did it come out years ago? Maybe. Is the information still relevant? Probably. Can you create three or five different social media posts around it and add it to your Content Stockpile?[31] Definitely.

By including this kind of content in your mix, your followers will start to know you better. They'll realize that you're a smart / inspiring / entertaining cookie and you will start to get more subscribers to your blog, podcast, or YouTube channel.

But they won't do that if you just drop a link once on the day that your podcast comes out.

Look, I get it. It's like, "I just spent hours editing this video. Isn't that enough? Do I also have to make a

---

[31] You'll learn about a Content Stockpile in Part III.

bunch of little pieces of content from it to put out on social?!"

The fact of the matter is, yes. Yes. You do. I do. We all do.

Exercise: What are five pieces of content that you can turn into Articles content?

_____

_____

_____

_____

_____

To see examples of Articles content, head to *simplesocialmediabook.com.*

Benefits of posting Articles content

Reasons to include Articles content in your content mix:

- It's usually evergreen. Repurposing it saves you coming up with something new.
- If you were a guest on a podcast, podcast hosts and producers love when you are willing to share the episode you were on multiple times. That is doing some of their job for them and a good reason for them to invite you back.
- This kind of content builds authority. It shows your audience that you know what you are talking about.
- If it's your own video, podcast, or blog, you are pointing people back to your website.

Remember, you're not just posting your newest article once. You are creating multiple posts to stockpile[32] so that you can regularly cycle through them whenever you post Articles content.

---

[32] More on varying content in Part III.

The *SNL* "Best of Dana Carvey" strategy

Even if you haven't updated your YouTube channel, blog, or podcast in a while you can still create Articles social media posts from it. You just may have to think about your posts or episodes in a different way.

When I was growing up, it was common for *Saturday Night Live* to put together a "best-of" compilation of sketches featuring one of its popular cast members—past or present—and air it in prime time.

This was great for NBC because they could still have programming when a show was on hiatus. It was great for SNL because it could highlight what they were doing when much of that audience was asleep. It was great for the performers because it raised their profiles. And it was great for my brother and me because we could watch SNL on a school night.

You could package your own best-of posts or episodes and then highlight them on social media in your Articles category.

Here are some "packages" for you to think about. Put together five of these, make images for each post within the bundle, and share them as a carousel of images in your Articles category.

- Most recent
- Most viewed of all time
- Most clicked of all time
- Collection based around one topic (like productivity tips)
- Guest posts round-up
- Top posts of the year (end-of-year round-up)
- Posts based on a specific author

Get creative! If you find yourself saying, "I dunno. I haven't updated my YouTube channel in a while," my guess is, you could cull what you already have and repurpose it throughout your social media. And when you do that, schedule them for Articles day.

If you don't have a podcast / YouTube channel / blog

If you don't have some kind of long-form content, first, I'd consider creating one. If nothing else, it makes it very easy to repurpose and use in a myriad of ways.

Long-form content is great for search engine optimization, helps you deepen relationships with your audience, and hones your voice so you can differentiate yourself. Having people in your industry be a guest on your podcast, show, or blog is also a great way to get to know them.

Here's a method I've used for years with clients so they would have a simple way of creating long form content that we could repurpose:

1. Go live on YouTube once a month and talk about a topic in your niche.[33]

2. Come up with four questions your audience might ask about that topic (or already has asked about that topic).

3. Answer each one of the four questions in the video.

4. Edit each one of those answers into four bite-sized videos that you can post on social.[34]

When I would do this with my clients, it would take about forty-five minutes. We would budget fifteen minutes for what I called a "tech check" and then go live for about twenty or thirty minutes, depending on the topic or the guest.[35]

---

[33] It doesn't have to be live, but when it is live, you do much less editing. Video editing is an enormous time suck. I've used Be.Live, Streamyard, and Wave.video to livestream. All great streaming platforms in their own ways.

[34] In the time between my starting to write this book and it being published, a myriad of artificial intelligence tools have come out that do this exact task. I'll be keeping a running tally of my favorites in the resources at *simplesocialmediabook.com*.

[35] If you really want to maximize this content, you can turn a recap of it into a blog post and embed the YouTube video into it. But on the other hand, I don't want you or Avril Lavigne coming after me asking, "Why you gotta go and make things so complicated?"

If you don't have the bandwidth to do that sort of thing, you can share content other people have created and add your two cents. In the biz, we call this "curated content." And it will save you so much time.

Find YouTube videos, podcast episodes, blog posts, or articles that someone else has written and share them to your social media feed. Make sure that you insert your point of view, so that your audience can learn what that is.[36] By doing this, you can keep a steady stream of content on your feed that is good-quality, curated content that you didn't have to create, but merely comment on.

To be clear, I am not suggesting that you pass off other people's ideas as your own. You are going to share the content that someone else has published. I recommend that you tag the author and the company that published it. You may be able to get into a dialogue with them about the piece itself.

Over time, though, start to create some kind of long form content on your own.

To see an example of Articles content, head to *simplesocialmediabook.com*.

---

[36] And actually, so can you!

Simple Truth:

People respond
to accounts that
are up-to-date.

Promotional
Articles

General

Engagement
Random

The PAGER method:
General content

General Content is the "G" of the PAGER method. I like to think of it as the O.G. of social media content.[37]

These are the kinds of posts that you've most likely been putting up consistently on your channels already. General content is meant to inspire, entertain, and/or educate your followers. Not only are General posts designed to show what you know and who you are, they also show your audience that you get them. You understand what their struggles are. You understand what's going to be a win for them. It's an opportunity for you to show your authority and show empathy.

---

[37] Yes, of course I included "O.G. Original Gangster" by Ice-T on the PAGER Method Mixtape. And, yes, you can hear the whole playlist at *simplesocialmediabook.com*. I live to serve.

General content includes posts that are:

- Beliefs / values / motivations
- Case studies / social proof / stories / testimonials
- Holiday or hashtag-holiday oriented
- Industry event oriented
- Memes / mumor
- Problems / solutions / tips / myths / objection crushers
- Rants / raves

Ever since social media began, critics have said that there is simply too much navel gazing. At first, people would lament how it seemed everyone was posting what they had eaten for lunch, and now people take umbrage with how much content is so self-absorbed.

General content, with the PAGER method, combats those criticisms.

When you publish posts for your brand or project, create content that revolves around your audience. Put out pictures, videos, or Stories that let them know instantaneously that your account is for them and is valuable to them. It's more than a bunch of selfies. By following you, they get inspired, entertained, or educated in the stuff that they care about.

To see examples of General content, head to *simplesocialmediabook.com.*

You've got substance . . . now add *style*

A guest chapter by copywriter Paige Worthy

Ready to start scheduling? Not so fast!

Having the content is one (important) thing. But sharing it in a way that makes Your People pop out of their holes like meerkats? That's the good stuff.

So before you pop outta that cocoon, you little social butterfly, it's time to get your brand voice all the way together. Let's create a handy brand voice reference for you and your team!

But why?

In a perfect world, your content will be so seamless that nobody will know you've got multiple team members (or an outside contractor, or AI, or your very smart cat) working on your social content. Even the briefest style guide sets you up for consistent authenticity. Boom!

Here's what to include:

General brand overview

Anyone working on your social content should know exactly what you're about. This is a great place for . . .

- A bullet-point brand narrative
- Your Big Why
- Your mission or vision statement
- What role you play in your ideal customer's world

We are . . . we're not

Imagine if one of your followers were telling someone about your rad social presence. What are some adjectives you'd want them to use to describe you? What are some descriptors that would make you cringe?

Pick a few on either side of the aisle, then create a section like this:

We Are:	We're Not:
Irreverent We surprise our community with off-the-cuff content that inspires snort-giggles and tons of Story shares.	*Crass* We don't do gross-out humor, and we don't share content that gets laughs at anyone else's expense.

You could even include examples of dos and don'ts.

A celeb doppelganger

If your brand asked an A-lister to do a one-day social takeover, who would you pick, and why? Is there someone already in the public eye whose own brand personality and voice could rep your brand to a T? Pop in a couple of solid-gold screen-shots for good measure.

Your sense of humor

How does "funny" work its way into your social content? Remember, there's not just one way to get a chuckle:

- Corny / dad jokey
- Nerdy
- Punny / wordplay
- Sarcastic
- Dark
- Esoteric

Bonus points, as always, for examples.

Note: You actually don't *have* to be laugh-out-loud funny. Content that educates, moves, inspires, or just plain makes people smile is plenty.

Catch-all style tips

What else should someone creating content for you know in order to sound consistently authentic? For example . . .

- Does queer slang, AAVE, or regional flavor make its way into your content?
- What about emojis or nah?
- Are there any jokes your social audience is in on? (We love a good callback.)
- Did you learn the hard way to cool it on certain "yikes" topics? (Caches can be cleared and tweets deleted, but the memory of the internet is astounding.)

Your best social content

Finally, if you've been on the socials for a minute, grab a smattering of screen-shots of posts that have done well across various platforms. Then share why they did so well and explain how your brand personality contributed to their success! These are the building blocks for more successful social content.

Teamwork makes the dream work

An engaging social presence doesn't happen by accident. If you're going to be intentional about creating a content strategy for social, put the same intention toward the voice you'll use to put it all out there.

* * *

Get Paige Worthy's *Win Hearts With Words* brand voice guide. You'll learn fifteen copy tweaks that will make strangers fall in love with your brand voice. Head to *paigeworthy.com/win-hearts-with-words*.

Software for creating General content right now

The PAGER method was designed after nearly ten years of paying attention to the social media space. I have seen trends come and go. And I built PAGER with what didn't seem to change over that time.

But, nonetheless, it's important to capitalize on trends when you can—especially when you're talking about unpaid social media posts. If you want to get your posts seen, you've got to pay the platforms. If you don't want to do that, you've got to play the game a little bit.

I've put together a list of my favorite tools for creating General content. I was going to mention them in the book, but the tools kept coming and going. While I was writing this book, Twitter changed a bunch, and as a result many of those tools became moot.

Suffice it to say, that in the fast-paced world of social media, this list rapidly changes. You can get a list that will consistently update at *simplesocialmediabook.com.*

Simple Truth:

People respond to content that is about them.

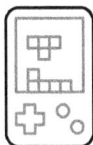

The PAGER method:
Engagement content

On social media, we all have one goal. And the Goo Goo Dolls said it best: "I just want you to know who I am."

The "E" of the PAGER method is for Engagement. These are the posts that help build your relationship with your audience because you are asking them for their opinion. And if there's anything social media has taught us, it's how to express an opinion.

Engagement posts encourage your audience to comment, tap, slide, or somehow or other respond to your posts. You want to make sure that you include these in your content mix for a few reasons.

The first is that you want your audience to know how much you value their thoughts and opinions.

What better way to let your audience know that you value their opinion than by asking them what it is?

Another reason why it's important to include this type of post is because when someone taps, slides, comments, or shares a post of yours, that person is more likely to see your content in the future.

Not only that, but often algorithms will only show your posts to a small subset of your followers— the most engaged ones. When those followers react in some way to them, then the social media platform will show your content to a larger group of your followers.

So in order to get more mileage out of your posts, you want to make sure that you regularly are posting content designed to get your audience talking.

Engagement posts can be:

- Polls
- Sliders
- Answer with a GIF
- Answer with an emoji
- This or that
- Open-ended questions

- Games

When Engagement posts go wrong

The problem with posting this kind of content too often is that it can start to feel annoying to your audience after a while. It can feel a little needy. People may start to think, why are they asking *me* so many freaking questions all the time?

With the PAGER method, though, you are only posting this type of content 20% of the time, so you can be sure that it's not overkill.

Remember, you have Promotional content as part of your PAGER system, so you do have another post throughout the week designed to help you hit your business goals.

Note: I like to post Engagement content on Friday afternoons or at any time that I think my audience could use a little levity. Just make sure that you are ready to field any of the responses that come in. So if you publish an Engagement post on Friday afternoon, make sure that you aren't going off social for the weekend.

To see examples of Engagement content, head to *simplesocialmediabook.com*.

Using AI with Engagement content

I'm old school and grew up in a time when there was a set of encyclopedias[38] in every classroom. It was drilled into me that when you use an article from an encyclopedia, for example, you have to cite it.

I still have an inclination to do that. Even when I've paid for a social media course and it includes a list of open-ended questions, I always felt a little weird about using them without citing the source. And

---

[38] Children, an encyclopedia was a set of books about many different topics (think Wikipedia). Every year it would be updated. But instead of being written by literally anyone, they were written by experts and then fact checked. Imagine. Having a source of information that was written by professional writers, based on facts, and then checked by actual fact checkers.

then I felt even weirder about handing that same list to a client of mine who hasn't bought the course.

I hate to take someone else's ideas and pass them off as mine. Using questions that were generated by a computer—sentient robot?—puts the student in me at ease. And then I can go and save myself a boatload of time by creating a number of different posts based on a topic in my niche that is meant for my audience.

In the time that I have started writing this book, artificial intelligence has exploded. By the time that you are reading this book, odds are good that you have already played with it a bit and have worked it into your day-to-day operations.

But here's a great way to use it with PAGER, specifically with Engagement content.[39]

Note: I specifically like to use Jasper.ai for this, but I'm sure by now there are a myriad of other tools that you can use.

---

[39] Quick note about AI: just like you would with a template, obviously don't blindly copy and paste the outputs. It can get really weird if you do. Look with a critical eye to make sure that what comes out sounds not only like a human but also sounds like you. And check the spelling. Believe it or not I found a spelling error in an output one time.

Here are prompts to use:

Topic: Use a topic idea from your cache of General posts.

Example: Time is our most important asset.

Audience: Define your audience.

Example: Mompreneurs

Quick tip: Distill your Brand Voice into a few words to use when you are crafting prompts for your Engagement posts. To uncover your tone of voice, copy and paste a snippet from a newsletter or blog post you wrote. Or, if you want to get really authentic, a transcript of a podcast episode, or video you've created.

Example: Helpful and instructional

You'll get a bunch of responses that come up that you can copy and paste and use in your social media. You can also turn those same questions into square images for your Instagram feed, and Stories too. For every response you get, aim to create three pieces of content around it.

Using AI to come up with engaging questions for your audience will help you put out a lot of content in a very small amount of time. So that you can spend more time interacting with your audience.

Promotional

Articles

General

Engagement

Random

The PAGER method:
Random content

"R," the final letter in PAGER, stands for Random. This means that you choose any content from any of your other categories and have it go out. It can also stand for Repurpose. Or Reuse.

If you have an event coming up, this is where you may post about it a couple of times in the week.

Here's how it works the best with social media schedulers: If you already have your content labelled "Promotional," "Articles," "General," or "Engagement," you can also mark it as "Random.". So when you create a Random time slot, that content will go out.

If you don't have a Random option on your third-party scheduler, some ideas are:

- Reschedule a post that did well a few months ago.
- Share someone else's post.
- Choose a Promotional post for something coming up soon.
- Publish an Articles post for a podcast episode, blog post, or video that needs a little love.

For a list of up-to-date schedulers that have this feature, head to *simplesocialmediabook.com*.

Play the hits

My dad, Bill Figenshu, is a retired radio guy.[40]
He was the head of Viacom's radio division and
launched some of the most successful radio stations
of all time.[41] One of his secrets? "Play the hits."

Dad is a firm believer in finding what works and
giving it to your audience. And your social media
can do that too.

So often you think you have to come up with new
ideas to turn into social media posts. But you don't.

And you don't have to. Instead, you can take content
from before and repurpose it. Like when an artist

---

[40] There were always the best hits of the '80s, '90s, and today
playing in my house growing up.

[41] Radio Ink magazine named him one of the 40 most powerful
people in radio in 2001.

will release an unplugged version of a song.[42] You can also just . . . replay the content.

You can just take a post from three months ago, or six months ago, or a year, and have it go out again.

Like, do you think Taylor Swift came up with all new songs for her Eras Tour? No. She is playing songs that other people have heard before because they know them and they have responded to them.

When you're creating content, don't come up with a new concept. Just repurpose it: change up the visuals; adjust the copy; update the format.

Or not. Just put it out again. Either way:

Play the hits.

---

[42] Children, there was a magical time in the '90s and early 2000s when MTV had a series called MTV *Unplugged* and musical acts would perform their songs acoustically. Highlights include Nirvana's "All Apologies" and Jay-Z's "H to the Izzo."

Don't just schedule— automate

Automation is an important piece of the puzzle in terms of setting you free, time-wise.

There is a difference between scheduling social media posts and automating them.

Scheduling them means that you say to your scheduler:

> *Publish this Articles post on LinkedIn on Thursday, May 18th at 11AM.*

Automating them means that you say to your scheduler:

> *Publish one of these Articles posts on LinkedIn on Thursdays at 11AM.*

The posts will go out without your having to sit there and figure out every Thursday at 11AM.

Resources that have this capability:[43]

- Cloud Campaign
- CoSchedule
- MeetEdgar

By automating the posts that you've created, and made a few variations for, you don't have to feel like you are tethered to your desk making social media posts. You can take a week or two off if you need to.

I have found this really comes in handy when:

- You want to go on vacation.
- You are starting to feel burnt out and need a break.
- You have a big project that you're going to be heads-down on.
- Your childcare / eldercare situation changes and you need to be more hands on.

---

[43] As of this printing, of course. And subject to change. But I always keep this list up to date at *simplesocialmediabook.com*.

By automating your content, all you have to do is pop in to respond to comments when they come up, or allocate that simple task to someone else.

Agency case study for PAGER

A guest chapter by Matt Banker of Benchmark Growth

It's kind of embarrassing for a marketing agency to be so bad at their own social media. But that was the exact situation we were in.

Our social media strategy revolved around developing me (the owner) as a thought leader on marketing for accounting firms. I never had an issue generating ideas. My problem was my posting was sporadic and lumpy.

I would wait until inspiration would strike, typically once every couple of weeks at 8PM on a Sunday. Then I'd crank out four to five posts at once and hit "publish." Naturally, they would get little engagement because no one is on LinkedIn on a Sunday evening.

So those brilliant nuggets of wisdom would sink to the bottom of the algorithm, never to be seen again.

I tried posting right when I got to work each day, but I'm not the type of person that thrives on routine like that. I was also too busy (or too disinterested?) to take the time to repurpose other content we were creating for social media, so some of our best stuff was essentially invisible.

Using the PAGER method turned social media into a team sport for us. Here's what we did.

We used the Brandscript + dice method[44] to generate a library of promotional text posts, and our designer created portfolio highlights for PIE content.

My VA and copywriter were tasked with creating posts for the blog content and podcasts we were producing for Articles content.

We built our General content around the posts I was already writing, and our designer would take my best performing text-based posts and create graphic versions of them.

---

[44] More on that soon.

And we employed a team effort to create Engagement content (this is still probably still our weakest area). All of our content fed directly into a social media automation software to drip out different categories of content throughout the week. Rather than posting directly on social media at random times or trying to choose a perfect time to schedule each individual post, it freed us up to focus on consistently producing good content.

I tell my clients all of the time: Published is better than perfect. We needed a framework that would allow us to spread out responsibility for our social media activity, be consistent in our posting, and maintain a high level of authority, and PAGER did that for us.

Another way of saying this is: the best plan is the one that you can execute. What I love about the PAGER method is that it's a plan that we can actually follow.

* * *

You can find out more about Benchmark Growth at *marketingforaccountingfirms.com*.

PART III

Implementing the PAGER Method

Simple Truth:

Overthinking can lead to overreaching. Start simple.

From Under Pressure to Ice Ice Baby

At this point, you understand why you need to have simple social media. And you understand what the PAGER method is and what automation is.

Now, it's time to discuss how to implement the PAGER.

True, I have trained marketing agencies and their social media teams on the PAGER method, but in the interest of simplicity, I am going to break down how we have found it works for one company. It is almost identical to the process that we use at Downstage Media for our clients.

Compared to the alternatives of posting four or five times a week whenever and however you can, one of the biggest differences that Downstage Media's clients and content creators have experienced is more time freedom.

For example, after the first eight weeks, at any time there is at least a month of posts that are already in the can. So when the content creator went away for a long weekend, when a client had a sudden family situation, the posts kept going out, and the relationship-building activities could continue. As content creator and manager Michelle Markey said, "The PAGER method is genius and has helped me free up time and have more ease in my workflow."

Let's give you that experience too!

How to figure out which social media platforms to focus on

You know that it's going to be too hard to handle more than two social media platforms at any one time. So you've got to get strategic about which ones you are going to focus on. This exercise will help you do just that.

Where are you currently posting?

Make a list of the social media platforms that you currently are posting to on a regular basis.

Of these, which play to your brand's strengths the best?

Although many features of social media platforms overlap,[45] there are some that lend themselves more to certain types of content.

Of these, where is your audience active and spending their time?

Which platforms do you get the most comments on? If it's pretty much crickets across the board then ask yourself where your audience is likely to be.

Of these which works best with your workflow?

If you don't have time to edit videos—and don't want to hire someone else to do it—then don't look at one of the more video-forward platforms.

Once you've answered these questions, you should have one or two platforms left to build your audience on.

And guess what? That's enough! That's okay! That is manageable! That's sustainable. That's simple.

---

[45] They all have some live video component, for example.

Quick thing: If possible, try not to have both of them be under the same ownership. For example, Meta owns Facebook, Instagram, and Threads. So avoid putting all your eggs in the Meta basket. Should there be an issue with your account, you want to make sure that your brand is diversified.

How to deal with the accounts that you already have that you're not going to focus on

Now that you know which two social media accounts you're going to focus on, you've got to do something with your other social media accounts that you're not going to focus on.

Here are some options:

You can make them dormant. Most platforms have a way that you can hide the account without actually deleting it. Should your team expand and you have more bandwidth for that platform, for example, you can just reactivate it.

Some platforms may not allow you to hide or deactivate the accounts. You have to delete them outright. If you're not ready to do that yet, then you can create a post that says that you're not going to be posting on this account anymore. Share where you are going to be active. Pin the post to the top of your feed. This way, you don't look like you just abandoned an account. Your audience knows where to find you. And you can move on to bigger and better things.

How to use a BrandScript to create Promotional social media posts

To create Promotional posts quicker, start with a group of talking points that you can base your posts on. Using a BrandScript ensures you have all of the pertinent pieces of information that an audience member will need in order to make a purchasing decision. For social media, you're not going to use all of the elements of the BrandScript in your posts. But you'll want to touch on a few of them. First, though, let's get into what a BrandScript is.

A BrandScript is a collection of messages that you draw from in order to make marketing assets.

Just like how a script contains the words that the actors say throughout a film, a BrandScript contains the words that your brand uses throughout its marketing.

Donald Miller came up with the concept and wrote about it in his book *Building a StoryBrand*. He can also walk you through the process in his StoryBrand Messaging Framework course in Business Made Simple.[46]

Honestly, a BrandScript is a glorified outline, so if you went to the kind of school that taught grammar and diagramming sentences and proper outline structure[47] you're going to find using a BrandScript both helpful and familiar. If you didn't go to that kind of school then you'll find using a BrandScript to be mind-blowingly helpful.

---

[46] For a free 7-day trial of Business Made Simple, with the Building a StoryBrand online course, head to *simplesocialmediabook.com*. The Building a StoryBrand online course will walk you through how to make your own BrandScript.

[47] Kids, there used to be a thing called grammar and it was taught in schools so you would have a command over the language. But when texting and Twitter became a thing, we as a country just gave up and now we're lucky if children are taught capitalization.

Once you get the hang of them, you can fire them off quickly.

I recommend creating a BrandScript for:

- Your overall brand
- Each division of your company
- Every product that you offer
- Each lead generator that you create
- Upcoming events
- Initiatives your company has coming up
- Each blog post / podcast episode / YouTube video you create

The great thing about a BrandScript is that you can hand it off to whoever is making your marketing assets and you know that they will use already-approved messages.

So if you hired someone to create your social media posts for you, you can tell them to create five posts based on your upcoming event, hand that person the BrandScript for the event, and you can trust that the messaging you want is going to be consistent across all of your social media channels.

How to use dice and a coin to make Promotional content

To make a batch of Promotional social media posts efficiently, use your BrandScript and pull two of the talking points from it plus a call to action.

Because at Downstage Media we are making this kind of content all of the time, I turned it into a dice game you can play to make the posts go faster.

One social media manager for an accounting firm told me that he created ten posts in thirty minutes using this method. He was thrilled! Here's how you can do the same:

1. Create a BrandScript for your promotion, initiative, or event.

2. Number it from 1-10 like the image you'll find at *simplesocialmediabook.com*.

3. Roll a 10-sided die (Google has a free online version) twice.[48]

4. Write copy that corresponds to numbers that you've rolled on your BrandScript.

5. Add an image, link, or video.

6. Repeat until you have five posts created for each Promotion, Initiative, or Event your brand is currently promoting.

For a downloadable numbered BrandScript and a video to see this process in action, head to *simplesocialmediabook.com*.

---

[48] t's always fun when I lead Simple Social Media workshops to see who are the Dungeons and Dragons people in the crowd who already have access to 10-sided dice. No shame, though. As a musical theater geek, I don't run in those circles, but I respect them.

Simple Truth:

Everyone needs kindness and support. Especially online.

How to pop in on social media and make it count

On *Seinfeld*, Elaine, Kramer, and George all loved "popping in" on Jerry at his apartment. When you are short on time, a pop-in is just the right thing to do on social media—especially if you are starting to feel like you haven't posted enough recently. With the pop-in, you can actually start building real relationships with the people that you are connected to on social media.

There are two main ways that you can pop in whenever you open up one of your social media apps. By using this technique, I was able to increase the number of accounts I reached on Twitter from 9,000 to 30,000 in sixty days.

I'll break down each one and why they're
so beneficial.

By doing these every day you'll start to develop
real relationships with people—and with
their audiences.

#1: Share something someone else has done

"Retweet." "Share." "Stitch." Every social media
platform has its own language, and every social
media platform has a way to take what someone
else has created and place it in front of your
audience. It's how content goes viral.

Every time you go on social media, share a piece of
content someone else has posted and add your two
cents. Here's why:

1. You don't always have time to create content.
   By sharing someone else's post you are keeping
   your account fresh without having to do any of
   the actual content creation.
2. Your audience will appreciate that you are
   consistently putting out entertaining, inspiring,
   or educational stuff on your feed whether or
   not you created it. And that you always add
   your personal color to it.

3. Everyone who puts content out wants it to be shared further. It's validating. By sharing someone else's content, they see that you are in their corner.

4. The algorithms will like that you are consistently posting.

Tip: Use your powers for good. If you are going to share someone's point of view that you disagree with, be kind, gracious, and thoughtful in expressing your differing opinion. Lead with empathy here. Life is hard enough without having to worry about people dragging us down on the internet because we have a different idea about something that's probably not even going to matter in three weeks anyway.

#2: Comment on other people's posts

This is another super simple technique that will yield excellent dividends.

We all like receiving comments on our posts, but we don't always leave comments on other people's posts. So when you give a kind, gracious, or thoughtful opinion on other people's posts, that matters to them and their audiences.

And by doing so, you'll start to build allies. People will want to be in your corner because you're starting to be in theirs.

Bonus? Your comment will get in front of their audience. Which means your account will get in front of their audience.

So if you wanted to get a little strategic about this you could:

1. Follow the accounts in your niche that have larger followings than you do, so your account gets in front of their audiences.
2. Follow the accounts of rock stars in your niche so you start to build a relationship with their audiences.
3. Follow the accounts of people you want to work with so you can get to know one another. (Be careful with this one. Don't be weird. Remember, be kind, gracious, and thoughtful.)
4. Follow the accounts of people you are working with so they know that you are in their corner.
5. Follow the accounts of the people who work for you so they know that you value them.

If you are rushed, though, just make a kind, gracious, and thoughtful comment on someone's post and move along with your day.

Simple Truth:

"You're not a nobody,
but you need friends."
— David Newman

Relationship-building activities

Putting out content is great.

But where you really get to know *people* is by spending time building relationships. This is the *social* part of social media.

You know how sometimes business coaches will tell you that you need to focus on income producing activities? They'll say to make sure that you are doing some IPAs every day?

Well, these are RBAs: relationship-building activities.

Set a timer for fifteen minutes, and do as many of these as you can get to, in the order that they appear. If you aren't able to do that task (like if you don't have any comments today), then just skip it and go to the next one.

Here is a list of tasks to do in fifteen minutes on one or both of the platforms that you are building your audience on.

Note: Depending on the platform the terms may be slightly different ("repost" versus "share," for example) but you get the idea.

- Connect with someone who has commented on a post.
- Reply to a comment on the person's post.
- Like a post.
- Like a comment.
- Tag in one of your posts.
- Comment on a post.
- Repost with your thoughts.
- Repost.

Get in the habit of doing these tasks three times a week for fifteen minutes at a time. This will help you build relationships with the accounts that are in your space, and get your account in front of more people to grow your audience.

All of these tasks are organized according to social media platform and available to make your own in the Relationship-Building Activities template that you will find in the resources at *simplesocialmediabook.com.*

Allies, influencers, clients, customers: the people in your neighborhood

One tactic to use, is to keep a list of "the people in your neighborhood."

There was a *Sesame Street* song when I was a kid that asked the question, "Who are the people in your neighborhood?" and that's what inspired this tactic.

Well, that, and I had a client who was a local business and we would often comment and share the posts from the other businesses in the plaza that her studio was located in. It became a nice way to show support for other local businesses, and they were happy to then share and comment on our posts too.

If you are a solopreneur who works out of your tiny little home office[49] then you may not have the same kind of neighbors.

In any event, start thinking about the people and the accounts that are in your world:

- Whom do you work with?
- Whom do you work for?
- Who are members of societies that you are a member of?
- Who holds certifications that you hold?
- Who is in the same or adjacent fields as you?
- Who are the rock stars in your industry?
- Who are the people that you would love to collaborate on a project with someday?

And when you work on your RBAs, sing that song from *Sesame Street* and remember that you are a business. And so many brands on social media are just tiny businesses trying to get off the ground and could use a little support.

Find the ones that are in your circle, and give them that support by commenting on their posts and sharing their posts and adding your two cents.

---

[49] Girl, same!

Note: Another great tactic to try is to collaborate with the people in your neighborhood. Maybe you are going to do an Instagram Live with them to talk about something that is happening in your niche. Maybe you could co-sponsor an event together.

One of my mentors, David Newman, says, "You're not a nobody, but you need friends." By relying on the people in your neighborhood, supporting them, and working together with them, you can help build up one another's social media presence.

Why showing your personal life on social media matters (and how to do it right!)

A guest chapter by Ashley Falletta

In the world of social media for business, people often forget that the ultimate objective is to make and maintain connections. It's called "social" media for a reason!

Connection real estate is precious (and sometimes limited) to your target audience, so if you want to forge a relationship with your ideal client, you need to let them know the real you, the face behind the brand.

Sharing glimpses of your personal life can be intimidating and a gamechanger for your business. It humanizes your brand, fosters trust, and attracts an audience with the same values as yours and your business.

While sharing pictures of your coffee or morning routine can be fun, posting too much of your personal life can be a recipe for disaster. You don't want to risk diluting your professional image by lacking strategy behind your content.

So, how can you strike the right balance?

Read the room

Make sure you are clear on your ideal client and their psychological drivers. What types of things do they enjoy, and can you connect with them on a personal level with fun and engaging content? If you're not sure of the answer, use built-in platform features like polls, Q&As, and online forums to get to know your audience.

Engaging with them puts content consumption in their court, and fosters a sense of belonging and ownership in the brand community.

Be transparent

Authenticity is key to building trust with your audience. Share genuine moments that provide insights into your brand's journey, values, or processes. Be transparent about your successes and challenges to show that you are a human living an everyday life, just like them. Also, show that you are open to addressing customer concerns with active social listening and accept feedback with grace and integrity. Honesty, above all, wins the day.

Have fun (while staying relevant)

Anything you post should be created with a growth strategy, but that doesn't mean it has to be boring. That being said, always ask yourself, "How is this moving my brand forward?" You may love to collect garden gnomes, but how does sharing this quirky hobby fit into your business landscape? Plan your content with an objection in mind: to inspire, to engage, to increase brand awareness, to drive traffic, to boost sales or build community.

Build relationships

Engage, engage, engage! Don't let your social media be one-sided. Communication should be your #1 priority. Respond to comments and DMs. Search keywords and hashtags in your industry and share your thoughts and support on what others are posting. To stand out even more, send voice notes or personalized video messages on the platforms that support these features. Show your followers some love and let them know their support is appreciated.

Professionalism is paramount

Remember, you're running a business, not a reality TV show. Keep your personal life from overshadowing your brand. Save the wild nights and breakup rants for your close pals and therapist, and never speak poorly about anyone else online (or off!). While fleeting, these overshares live on the internet forever and can come back to haunt you at any time in your entrepreneurial or personal journey.

Balancing your personal life as a business owner can be daunting and a bit scary, but it can be done. Share enough to connect but not so much that it overwhelms your followers. You want to move them naturally from "intrigued to interested to invested" in your brand, and you can do this by positioning yourself as a guide who is living their best life, just like them.

* * *

For more from Ashley, head to *ashleyfalletta.com*.

How to create, vary, automate

What makes the PAGER method work so well is having a big pile of content that you can schedule. Then, once posts are going out, you simply have to respond to comments and DMs (like we talked about in the previous chapters) and add some new posts into the mix. And then, once a month, add in a few new pieces of content.

The simple way of creating that big stockpile of content is by varying the content that you are creating so you don't have to come up with as many new ideas. We have already talked about what kind of content to create (Promotional posts, Articles posts, General posts, and Engagement posts), so let's talk about how to vary them.

Let's get into what that looks like in the day-to-day.

For repurposing content, look to Disney

If you're thinking that coming up with different ways to say the same thing can be tricky, think about Disney's movie *Frozen*.

Frozen came out in 2013. The year that my oldest daughter was three. I can't tell you how pervasive this movie was: the songs were constantly in our heads, and the movie was constantly on.

And I'm not just including my own family. I'm talking about pretty much anyone who had a child under the age of five in the entire United States.

This movie was *everywhere*. And Disney knew how to capitalize on it.

But I'm not going to talk about the myriad of ways that Disney made money on *Frozen*. I'm just going to talk about the ways that Disney repurposed the story or the characters into books. Because in 2013 and 2014 Disney approved the release of seventeen different books, many of them simply retelling the story of the original movie.[50] Then, in 2015 Disney released seventeen more.[51]

There is someone who was tasked with writing the twenty-sixth *Frozen* book. And that person had to think, "How can I tell this story in a new way?" That's what you're going to do with the ideas you convey in your social media posts.

You're going to come up with the idea. Then you're going to vary it a number of different ways to make it seem new and fresh.

You're going to use many of the same words and switch up the format, or you're going to switch up the words and keep the format the same.

---

[50] I know this because I owned a number of them and would read them over and over again to my toddlers until they had them memorized.

[51] Based on disney.fandom.com/wiki/Frozen_books. And, honestly, if the Disney fandom Wiki is wrong, I don't want to be right.

By doing this you are creating more content to feed the insatiable appetite of a social media platform.

Variation I: Same format, different message

Another way to vary your content is to change what you're saying, but keep it in the same format. Honestly, this is so simple, and I have no idea why people don't do it more often.

Let's say that you published a blog post, and now you want to point people towards it. (This would go in the Articles category.)

You want to write up a sentence or two, and then add the link to the blog post, then have it go out on LinkedIn.

You can come up with a few different variations and quintuple your output. Here's an example:

Variation I.1:

You explain why a sales funnel is just the first step. *downstage.media/blogindex/sales-funnel-steps*

Variation I.2:

You've built a sales funnel, but people aren't handing you their credit cards. Good news! Nothing is wrong. Read about the fundamentals all marketers know to nurture new audience members until they're ready to buy. *downstage.media/blogindex/sales-funnel-steps*

Variation I.3:

You've built your house with your messaging. Now invite guests into it with your marketing. Here are the simple fundamentals that all marketers know that will keep your brand in front of your audience until they're ready to buy. *downstage.media/blogindex/sales-funnel-steps*

Variation I.4:

The sales funnel can be running in the background while you're doing these other marketing tasks in the day-to-day. *downstage.media/blogindex/sales-funnel-steps*

Variation I.5:

Relying on social media solely for nurturing relationships with your audience is dicey since platforms can come and go so quickly. Coupling it with a solid email presence fortifies your efforts. *downstage.media/blogindex/sales-funnel-steps*

By coming up with a few different options to share what your blog post is about, and then stockpiling them, you can quintuple your social media output in minutes.

For formulas for varying your content, download the workbook at *simplesocialmediabook.com* so you can get a jump start on creating content.

Variation II: Same message, different format

One of the ways that we're going to simplify your social is to rein in the amount of stuff that you *think* you need to post about.

Many of my clients get overwhelmed with what sort of stuff to post because we have been told things like:

- "Anything can be content."

and

- "Document, don't create." [52]

And that is pretty much so open ended that I could just as easily be saying, "Post stuff! Lots of it! Constantly."

Um, what? First of all, we're not all camera-ready all the time, right? Second, if I did this, all my content would be me in my little home office. Not so visually interesting.

And another thing we have essentially been told:

- "Stop what you're in the middle of doing so you can post about it."

It's hard to get in the flow of what you're doing when you're taking yourself out of it to post about it. And numerous brain experts [53] have discussed how our brains aren't able to switch quickly from task to task. And doing so winds up wasting time because

---

[52] Look. I like Gary Vaynerchuk. He has always been very kind to me and very generous. We both own businesses in the same county in New Jersey! But "document, don't create" makes for a better soundbite than social media strategy. Also, it's way easier to document stuff when you have a social media marketing team documenting every move that you make, which he has. And which most brands do not.

[53] That's what they're called, right?

your brain has to get caught up with where it was in the task.

In psychology, the term for this is "switch costs." The American Psychological Association has studied research done in this arena and has deduced, "Although switch costs may be relatively small, sometimes just a few tenths of a second per switch, they can add up to large amounts when people switch repeatedly back and forth between tasks. Thus, multitasking may seem efficient on the surface but may actually take more time in the end and involve more error."[54]

So by making different posts throughout the day, you can be taxing your brain too much and costing yourself productivity.

And especially if I'm trying to do other things in my life—like run a business, participate in a family, eat—I don't want to be on my phone posting all of the time.

Instead, here's one simple solution to wrap your brain around: Post the same idea in different formats.

[54] apa.org/topics/research/multitasking

Let's say your brand is all about cleaning hacks and you want to give a quick glass cleaning tip. The idea might be:

Use coffee filters instead of paper towels to clean glass.[55]

And let's say that you are on Instagram. You can publish:

- A square image of someone[56] cleaning glass with a coffee filter
- A live video showing how to clean glass with a coffee filter
- A 30-second video showing how you can clean glass with a coffee filter
- A 90-second video detailing how you clean glass with a coffee filter and explaining which coffee filters in particular you find work really well
- A Reel with trending audio in the background while you clean glass with a coffee filter

---

[55] Apparently this is a thing. I worked in two restaurants— hours apart from one another—that both swore by this technique. One of them was a coffee shop at the Jersey shore, the other was a restaurant owned by a low-level Jersey mobster. Filters! Go figure!

[56] You, perhaps? A low-level Jersey mobster? You choose.

- A Story where you use the poll sticker to ask if anyone has ever used a coffee filter to clean glass

That's six different posts right there that are all based on the same idea.

Sure, you have to take the time to make all of the posts, but isn't it simpler to know that you're going to make six posts based on the same single idea versus six posts based on six different ideas?

Exercise: Come up with six different ideas that you can make posts about.

Justin Welsh does a great job of this concept with his Content Matrix which I first encountered in his LinkedIn Operating System. It's a rich course full of great tips that I recommend for anyone on LinkedIn. Also helpful for the artist formerly known as Twitter and Threads too. A link to it can be found in the free resources at *simplesocialmediabook.com*.

How to automate your content with the PAGER method

Scheduling posts is great so that you can decide what time and day each post is going to go out. So you can say, "Publish this post on Tuesday, July 12th on LinkedIn at 11AM." If you have a bunch of ten General posts, though, that can get a little tedious.

Automating, on the other hand, allows you to take that batch of ten posts and say, "Publish any of these posts on Tuesdays on LinkedIn at 11AM." It's an excellent way to free up time.

Here's how you can put your posts on autopilot.

1. Look for a scheduler that allows you to organize your posts by category and automate

them. MeetEdgar and Cloud Campaign do this, for starters.

2. Create a weekly schedule, incorporating one post every day from each letter of PAGER. (*Note:* They don't have to be in order.)

3. Take posts from your Content Stockpile and load them into your scheduler.

The content stockpile

With the PAGER method, you'll be creating triple or quintuple the number of posts you were making before. At Downstage Media, we deliver batches ten at a time to clients every two weeks. That's a lot of images, videos, and text to keep track of.

If you only upload them to your scheduler when you make them, you run the risk of not having a backup.

What happens, then, if one day you wake up and a giant social media platform has just taken over the account you've used for the past ten years to document your work and you don't have access to it anymore? Without any warning. Like the woman we talked about earlier who had the @metaverse handle on Instagram.[57]

---

[57] "Her Instagram Handle Was 'Metaverse.' Last Month, It Vanished." nytimes.com/2021/12/13/technology/instagram-handle-metaverse.html

Or, what happens if one day you wake up and a billionaire who recently took over the social media platform decides you're breaking the rules and kicks you off the platform? *Note:* He may or may not explain what the rules are that you broke.

Not only has this happened in the fifteen-year history of social media. Both of these occurrences happened in the *past two years.*

My point is that social media platforms are volatile. And if you're going to create great content to go on them, you want to make sure that you have all of that great content backed up.

Enter the *content stockpile.*

Rather than using a spreadsheet or putting a folder in Dropbox, create a content stockpile on a Trello board. That way the images and the videos can be stored together in a way that looks almost like how they will be on the platform.

I had a problem using spreadsheets because, although the content was organized, it wasn't visual. On the other hand, when I put videos or images in a Dropbox or Google Drive folder, I wouldn't have anywhere to keep the captions or the descriptions that would go with them. So it was disjointed.

With the content stockpile, you can:

- See all your posts in one place
- See all the variations of your post
- Easily ideate to create more post variations
- Back up your posts
- Share posts with anyone who may need to see them to give feedback or approvals
- Specify the exact date and time the post is going to go out (if necessary)
- Set alarms and reminders for anyone who needs to approve posts

As of this writing, there isn't an easy way for content from a Trello board (what I'm currently using to create the content stockpile) to automatically load up to MeetEdgar (my current social media scheduler).

Technology, though, is constantly changing. And with tools like Zapier that connect one app to another, it's worth it to potentially do the work twice, knowing that eventually the robots will be able to do it for you.

To pick up a Content Stockpile template, head to the free resources at *simplesocialmediabook.com.*

The "speak now or forever hold your peace" date

This section is for anyone who is creating content that needs approvals.

Whether or not you're paid for making posts, you want to make sure that someone else takes a look at them before they publish. Here's why:

- A second set of eyes is always helpful to spot typos and quality control.
- If there's any dustup, you can be assured that someone else has seen it ahead of time and has backed you up.

Sometimes you'll get those people who just don't care what you publish on their brand's social media channels. They are so happy that someone else has taken this over that they pass it off to you and don't look back.

Other people want to check and double check every single word, image, and URL.

Both of these types of people are great in their own ways and will make you better at what you do.

Here's the thing, though: Almost none of them realize how quickly social media moves.

One client, for instance, would require that she look at all posts before they were published. Which was great, but then she wouldn't actually take the time to look through them because she was too busy.

So then I was faced with a dilemma: If I don't schedule the posts, the algorithm is not going to like that a week or two has gone by without new material. So the number of accounts reached would go down, which reflects poorly on the work that I'm doing. On the other hand, I didn't want to publish posts without the client's permission.

So, I created what I call the "speak now or forever hold your peace" date. This is the date that I have to get approvals from the client.

At Downstage Media, we usually deliver them to the client with three business days to approve. So we notify them there is a batch on a Friday and the client has until the end of the business day on Wednesday to give us feedback. If they are too busy, though, the posts will go out anyway.

Note: This requires a great amount of trust between the two of you and professionalism on your part.

If it's a new client, you can show the client previous work that you've done that is on brand, is appropriate, and shows your style.

If you're new to the world of social, then you must make sure that your posts are always appropriate and on brand and not take advantage of the logins and passwords that you've been given for this brand's account.

And . . .

If you say that you're going to have a batch of content for them to approve by a certain date, you must make those posts by that date.

You must make sure they have enough time to look through your batch of posts and give you feedback. Plus, enough time for you to make any adjustments, show those to the client, and still publish the posts on time.

Having a "speak now or forever hold your peace" date ensures that you, the client, and the algorithms have what you need to give a brand a consistent presence.

What's the deal with hashtags?

A guest chapter by Julia Block Pearson of Stratos Creative

You can recognize it as a phrase that has a "#" symbol before it. It is a soft link within a social platform to similar or trending topics or ideas. A good hashtag strategy is essential to helping new followers find your content.

Recommended implementation varies across each platform. Twitter recommends one or two whereas Instagram allows up to thirty. The key is to include enough hashtags to expand your reach without creating an overloaded post that could be flagged as spam. The primary way to avoid this scenario is to only use strategic and relevant hashtags.

In order to find strategic hashtags, you'll want to research them ahead of time. There are several tools on the internet that can automate the research process for you, but I prefer manually searching them on the platform so I can see what my audience sees. Here are a few tips on how to research hashtags:

- List out keywords that your ideal customer might be searching for. Consider your services, products, industry, and location.
- Search those keywords behind the "#" symbol to see what posts are using the hashtag. Evaluate if the content is relevant to your post's topic.
- Follow the hashtags that those posts are using and see if they'd be useful to you.

I generally suggest using hashtags that have between 40,000 to 250,000 posts. Posts that use larger hashtags may get lost in the shuffle. Smaller hashtags may not provide the visibility you want. That being said, if you've found the perfect smaller hashtag for your post, use it! You never know—your ideal audience may be searching for it and come across your post.

A *word of caution:* There may be days you are tempted to throw a few random hashtags on a post right before it goes live. It's not worth it; a haphazard approach to hashtags is not only a waste of your time, but can also limit your reach. Once you've compiled some good hashtags, group them together by category so you can easily copy and paste a list of relevant hashtags into your posts when you're scheduling your content.

A well-executed hashtag strategy can be the key to exponentially expanding the reach of your content and growing your social media presence.

* * *

To get started with your hashtag strategy so your posts reach the right audience, download Stratos Creative Marketing's Hashtag Strategy Guide at *stratoscreativemarketing.com/hashtag-strategy-guide*

Timeline: When to implement each stage of PAGER

It is highly possible that in reading this book you realize that you would be better off hiring someone else to handle your social media. If that's the case, good for you! I support clarity.

(There's a list of questions that you can ask them at *simplesocialmediabook.com*.)

But if you do want to handle your own social media, here is a timeline to follow.

If you try to put all of this in place at once you can get overwhelmed quickly. Instead, gradually incorporate the different elements discussed in this book to your work flow.

Week 1:

- Figure out which two platforms you will be active on.
- Find a scheduler / automator that you will use.
- Create a brand playbook where you will keep all of your brand's logos, fonts, colors, and BrandScripts, or use the template at *simplesocialmediabook.com*.

Week 2:

- Create a content stockpile, or use the template at *simplesocialmediabook.com*.
- Figure out which sales, initiatives, or events you are going to make Promotional posts for.
- Make a BrandScript for them.
- Roll the dice and create five Promotional posts for each sale, initiative, or event.
- Put the batch of ten posts you've created into your content stockpile on Friday for approvals by Wednesday.

Week 3:

- Fill in the Relationship-Building Activities template from *simplesocialmediabook.com*.

- Begin doing relationship-building activities three times a week for fifteen minutes / platform.
- Schedule / automate all approved and edited Promotional posts one time a week for the next ten weeks.

Week 4:

- Keep doing RBAs at leastthree times a week for fifteen minutes / platform.
- Choose any two articles you've written, appeared in, or curated; long-form videos you've produced or appeared in; or podcast episodes you produced or appeared in.
- Create posts from them so you have ten Articles posts total.
- Put the batch of ten Articles posts you've created into your content stockpile on Friday for approvals by Wednesday.

Week 5:

- Keep doing RBAs at least three times a week for fifteen minutes / platform.
- Schedule / automate all approved and edited Articles posts one time a week for the next ten weeks.

Week 6:

- Keep doing RBAs at least three times a week for fifteen minutes / platform.
- Put a batch of ten General posts you've created into your Content Stockpile on Friday for approvals by Wednesday.

Week 7:

- Keep doing RBAs at least three times a week for fifteen minutes / platform.
- Schedule / Automate all approved and edited General posts 1x /week for the next ten weeks.

Week 8:

- Keep doing RBAs at least three times a week for fifteen minutes / platform.
- Put a batch of ten Engagement posts you've created into your Content Stockpile on Friday for approvals by Wednesday.

Week 9:

- Keep doing RBAs at least three times a week for fifteen minutes / platform.
- Schedule / Automate all approved and edited Engagement posts one time a week for the next ten weeks.

Week 10:

- Keep doing RBAs at least three times a week for fifteen minutes / platform.
- Reuse content from the past and begin scheduling Random content.

By the end of Week 10, you will be posting five times a week, and have at least three weeks of content "in the can" ready to go out on autopilot.

You can see how implementing the PAGER method is such a great way to have a social media presence without having that constant pressure to create posts.

Having a presence without the pressure

Now you have the information that you need to create a solid social media presence. The best part, though, is that you also have the tools to create that presence so you don't have the pressure that social media puts on all of us.

Recently, Downstage Media had a client who was ill for a couple of weeks. He wasn't able to view or approve any posts. Did that put us behind schedule? Was anyone scrambling trying to get content up or get content approved while someone else wasn't feeling well? No. We could simply tell the client, "Take your time. We've got at least a month of posts already scheduled. Rest."

Conversely, one of Downstage Media's content creators recently went on vacation for a few days. She was able to complete her RBAs at the beginning of the week before she left, and at the end of the week after she'd gotten home. And in the meantime, she could go away knowing that she had over three weeks of posts approved and scheduled. So she could actually enjoy her vacation.

Social media can be a part of your marketing plan that doesn't have to take up hours and hours every week if you don't want it to. And it doesn't have to take up a massive amount of headspace.

You make a few decisions. You make a few posts. You automate them. You get on with your business.

Now that you have read this book, you have a clearer understanding of how to move forward.

I wish you the best. And I look forward to connecting with you on social media.

About the Author

Annie Figenshu is a speaker, consultant, and marketer who works with small businesses who want to build relationships with their audience.

The owner of the marketing agency Downstage Media, Annie is a StoryBrand Certified Guide and Mailchimp Partner. She blogs weekly about email and social media marketing on Downstage.Media.

She has worked with solopreneurs, authors, investment capital firms, Off-Broadway shows, and financial tech companies.

Feel free to reach out to Annie. You can find her at *annie@simplesocialmediabook.com.*

Get your complete set of downloadable worksheets, bonuses and companion tools by visiting *simplesocialmediabook.com.*

Acknowledgements

Writing a book was not something I'd planned. Which, when one thinks of the amount of plans I make, is unusual.

To you, the reader. Thank you for taking the time to read through these ideas and think through them. To try them on and test them out. Your time is valuable, and I am grateful you spent it here.

Sanjeevanee Vidwans, thank you for telling me to have an Acknowledgements section in the first place. You remind me to stop and celebrate. I appreciate your friendship, advice, and being up for a bowl of ramen.

I'd like to thank each person in the StoryBrand Certified Guide community, *The Tilt* community, Mailchimp Partners, and the Experience Advisors. Whenever I spoke about writing a book, you rallied around me with your kindness and helpfulness.

An extra special thanks and hug to Marc Angelos, Ryan Dziadosz, Dave Hertig, and Macy Robison for taking extraordinary measures like reaching out to me and saying, "How can I help you with this?" When you are a first-time author, self-publishing, a simple question like that is extraordinary.

Joe Pulizzi and Robert Rose made writing a book seem easy. Like something anyone could do. You both gave me a "why not me" attitude. And here we are. You are mentors who help guide me every week in *This Old Marketing*, and have especially offered support in getting this book published.

David Newman, you showed me a path to getting *Simple Social Media* into more hands and got me thinking more deeply about how it fits into all of what I'd like to be doing for my own career and the growth of Downstage Media. I knew from the start of our working together I'd benefit immensely from your teaching.

From when *Simple Social Media* was in its outline phase, to when it was more colored in, Jeannie and Jonathan Bradshaw offered me their time and patience. When I was feeling vulnerable and unsure, you gave encouragement and text messages filled with exclamation points.

Jennifer Barden, Chris Kam, Jim MacLeod, Jeff Scherer, Kate Winter, and the team at Lulu Press. I am so appreciative that you added your talents to this book. Thank you for handling my oftentimes rushed and frenzied emails with grace.

Matt Banker, Julia Block, Ashley Falletta, and Paige Worthy: thank you for sharing your voice and your smarts with me and with the readers of this book.

My extended family, how insufferable I must have seemed for over a year jabbering on about "my book my book my book" in our group chat or at our family get togethers. You have always accepted me and my big dreams and ideas with love, excitement, and just the right amount of teasing. Family is everything. And I love you all.

And, finally, for Abbey and Penny. You were the reason I discovered early mornings to begin with. And now you are the reasons I take advantage of them. I love you forever.

www.ingramcontent.com/pod-product-compliance
Lightning Source LLC
Chambersburg PA
CBHW071656210326
41519CB00021BD/6599

* 9 7 9 8 9 9 2 5 2 0 6 4 4 *